PUG PRINCIPLES

PUG PRINCIPLES

Celebrating the Canine Credo

☙ WILLOW CREEK PRESS®

Published by Willow Creek Press, Inc.
P.O. Box 147, Minocqua, Wisconsin 54548

Photo Credits:

Masterfile:
p5 © Minden Pictures/Masterfile; p9 © Raoul Minsart/Masterfile; p17 © Jennifer Burrell/Masterfile; p21 © Minden Pictures/Masterfile; p26 © Minden Pictures/Masterfile; p33 © Minden Pictures/Masterfile; p34 © Minden Pictures/Masterfile; p37 © Raoul Minsart/Masterfile; p38 © Minden Pictures/Masterfile; p42 © Mark Leibowitz/Masterfile; p50 © Raoul Minsart/Masterfile; p54 © Noel Hendrickson/Masterfile; p73 © Gary Gerovac/Masterfile; p82 © Minden Pictures/Masterfile; p89 © Minden Pictures/Masterfile; p93 © Minden Pictures/Masterfile;

iStockphoto:
p6, p10, p13, p14, p25, p29, p30, p45, p46, p49, p53, p58, p62, p74, p77, p78, p81, p85

Shutterstock:
p2, p18, p41, p57, p61, p65, p66, p70, p90, p94, p96

Design: Donnie Rubo
Printed in Canada

ACCEPTANCE

Yesterday I was a dog. Today I'm a dog.
Tomorrow I'll probably still be a dog. Sigh!
There's so little hope for advancement.

—Snoopy

APPRECIATION

If your dog thinks you're the greatest person
in the world, don't seek a second opinion.

—Jim Fiebig

BONDING

We never really own a dog
as much as he owns us.

—Gene Hill

CLARITY

Some days you're the dog,
some days you're the hydrant.

—Unknown

CONTENTMENT

Contentment is not the fulfillment of
what you want, but the realization
of how much you already have.

—Unknown

DREAMS

If a dog's prayers were answered,
bones would rain from the sky.

—Old proverb

EASE

Old dogs, like old shoes, are comfortable.
They might be a bit out of shape and a little
worn around the edges, but they fit well.

—Bonnie Wilcox

ENTHUSIASM

What put the wiggle in a little dog's tail
I'd like to know!
That gay little wiggle, that glad little waggle—
How did it grow?

It starts in his mind and it runs out behind
To the tip of his tail, and then
That glad little waggle, that gay little wiggle
Begins all over again.

—Arthur Wallace Peach

EXPECTATION

He has promised to wait for me... whenever...
wherever, in case I need him. And I
expect I will—as I always have.

—Gene Hill

FIDELITY

Histories are more full of examples of
the fidelity of dogs than of friends.

—Alexander Pope

FLATTERY

Our dogs will love and admire the
meanest of us, and feed our colossal
vanity with their uncritical homage.

—Agnes Repplier

FORGIVENESS

The best part about owning a dog is
the way he loves you, even when you
are impatient with him and have no time
this morning for a game of tug-of-war.

—Unknown

FREEDOM

I think we are drawn to dogs because they
are the uninhibited creatures we might be if
we weren't certain we knew better.

—George Bird Evans

FRIENDSHIP

Money will buy a pretty good dog,
but it won't buy the wag of his tail.

—Josh Billings

FULFILLMENT

Occasionally in life there are those moments
of unutterable fulfillment which cannot be
completely explained by those symbols called
words. Their meanings can only be articulated
by the inaudible language of the heart.

—Martin Luther King, Jr.

FUN

The dog was created especially for
children. He is the god of frolic.

—Henry Ward Beecher

HARMONY

Just because man no longer understands
his place in the universe, don't let him
assume all God's creatures have
become equally confused and trivial.

—Bill Tarrant

HEAVEN

If there are no dogs in heaven, then
when I die I want to go where they went.

—Unknown

IMMORTALITY

A good dog never dies. He always stays. He
walks beside you on crisp autumn days when
frost is on the fields and winter's drawing near,
his head is within our hand in his old way.

—Mary Carolyn Davies

INEVITABILITY

The perfection of a life with a...dog, like the perfection of an autumn, is disturbing because you know, even as it begins, that it must end. Time bestows the gift and steals it in the process.

—George Bird Evans

INSISTENCE

Dogs feel very strongly that they should always go
with you in the car, in case the need should arise for
them to bark violently at nothing right in your ear.

—Dave Barry

INSTINCT

If your dog doesn't like someone
you probably shouldn't either.

—Unknown

INTELLIGENCE

If you think dogs can't count, try putting
three biscuits in your pocket and then
giving Fido only two of them.

—Phil Pastoret

INTIMACY

It requires the intimacy of daily living with
a dog to know the subtle quality of his
mind, the ham-smell of his ears, and that
his wet nose in your mouth tastes salty.

—George Bird Evans

IRONY

Properly trained, a man can
be a dog's best friend.

—Corey Ford

LAUGHTER

Dogs laugh, but they laugh with their tails.

—Max Eastman

LOVE

A dog is the only thing on earth that loves
you more than you love yourself.

—Josh Billings

NOBILITY

Grave eyes, grave bearing, dignity of kings;
The gentleness and trust as of a child;
The flawless poise that veils old savage things
But half-remembered from the vanished wild.

—C.T. Davis

OBEDIENCE

The difference between cats and dogs is,
dogs come when they are called, cats
take a message and get back to you.

—Unknown

PATIENCE

When you leave them in the morning, they stick
their nose in the door crack and stand there like
a portrait until you turn the key eight hours later.

—Erma Bombeck

PEACE

With him, I know a secret comfort and a private peace. He has brought me understanding where before I was ignorant.

—Gene Hill

PEDIGREE

My dog is half pit bull, half poodle. Not much
of a watchdog, but a vicious gossip.

—Craig Shoemaker

PERFECTION

God sat down for a moment when the dog was
finished in order to watch it, and to know it
was good, that nothing was lacking, that
it could not have been made better.

—Rainer Maria Rilke

PERSPECTIVE

If you get to thinkin' you're a person of some influence, try orderin' somebody else's dog around.

—Will Rogers

PLAY

We don't stop playing because we grow old;
we grow old because we stop playing.

—George Bernard Shaw

RESPONSIBILITY

Scratch a dog and you'll find a permanent job.

—Franklin P. Jones

SELFLESSNESS

The one absolutely unselfish friend that a man can
have in this selfish world, the one that never
deserts him, and the one that never proves
ungrateful or treacherous, is his dog.

—George Graham Vest

SIMPLICITY

They fight for honor at the first challenge, make love with no moral restraint, and they do not for all their marvelous instincts appear to know about death. Being such wonderfully uncomplicated beings, they need us to do their worrying.

—George Bird Evans

TACT

You can say any fool thing to a dog and the dog
will give you this look that says, 'My God, you're
RIGHT. I NEVER would've thought of that!'

—Dave Barry

TEMPTATION

Never trust a dog to watch your food.

—Unknown

THERAPY

There is no psychiatrist in the world
like a puppy licking your face.

—Ben Williams

UNDERSTANDING

No philosophers so thoroughly
comprehend us as dogs.

—Herman Melville

VALUES

No man can be condemned for owning a dog.
As long as he has a dog, he has a friend; and
the poorer he gets, the better friend he has.

—Will Rogers

WEALTH

Whoever said you can't buy
happiness forgot little puppies.

—Gene Hill

ZEAL

Why should we mourn your happiness? You burned
clear flame, while he who treads the endless march
of dusty years grows blind and choked with dust
before he dies, and has not lived so "long" in those
long years as you in your few, vibrant, golden months,
when, like spendthrift, you gave all you were.

—Unknown